Heart to Pen
❦
Pen to Pages

Heart to Pen ❧ Pen to Pages

A Collection of Poems
by Eboni Echols

♥Eboni Echols♥

Heart to Pen ❦ Pen to Pages
© 2023, Eboni Echols
ISBN: 979-8-218-29429-8

First Edition, 2023

Printed in the United States of America

Edited by Matthew Feinstein
Cover Design by Adam Martinez
Layout Design by Jim Dodson

Dedication

I dedicate this book to every writer whose words were never seen or heard.

I dedicate this book to every artist who never had a canvas to display their art.

I dedicate this book to every bookshelf.

I dedicate this book to single mothers who felt like giving up.

I dedicate this book to every woman who just wanted to be loved.

I dedicate this book to every person who cannot find the words to say.

I dedicate this book to anyone who has struggled with mental health issues and depression.

I dedicate this book to every woman who tried her best to be in healthy relationships but found herself, unfortunately, in a cycle of bad ones.

I dedicate this book to you.

Above all, I dedicate this book to God.

Acknowledgments

I give honor to God and acknowledge Him for being gracious and merciful. He saw fit to give me words to write. It is because of God that I completed this work within its content. Thank You, Abba Father!

Thank you to my amazing mom, Brenda, who has always supported me and prayed for me when I could not pray for myself. Her love for me has pushed me this far. My little angels here on earth Zylan, Zack, and Zayda whose eyes remind me of God's love for me. To my big little sister, Danielle, who has always told me everything would be alright. I love you dearly.

To my sister from another mother, Camari, you are amazing. You are beautiful on the inside and out. You have inspired me to write and take my time until I am ready. Our sister-ship is God-ordained; Grateful for you.

To my Season 10 CLI (Community Literature Initiative) community, Tommy Domino, and all of my Long Beach Chapter classmates/students, meeting with all of you every Saturday has been a blessing. Thank you to Hiram Sims for creating this program for poets and, giving me an opportunity to be a part of a historic community.

To the publisher, editors, designers, and everyone who had a part to play in the production of this book, thank you for believing in my visions, dreams, and most importantly, God's spirit of what He has given me to share and for providing me the platform to flow freely. I appreciate you using your gifts to bring this all together.

Last but not least, I acknowledge you, the reader, for supporting this book.

Contents

Preface

Heart to Pen / Pen to Pages consists of poems I have written over many years. This book contains some of my personal life experiences, struggles, trials, testimonies, and moments that gave me hope where God comforted me. Words downloaded in my spirit have helped me overcome many dark times. This book is a poetic Psalm that points to my resiliency in Jesus. Overall, I have found that despite what I have faced, God always provides a light for me to continue to see and persist. God has poured words into my spirit, reminding me not to give up. To continue to hope and don't lose my hope in Him. My faith in God has gotten me to this point. I hope you, the reader, can resonate with some of my experiences. I pray that your spirit is encouraged as you read through every page. I pray that God speaks to you as He has poured words into my heart, to the pen, and to these pages.

2 Corinthians 4:17 NIV

For our light and momentary troubles are achieving for us an eternal glory that far outweighs them all.

Blossom

Who told you that you weren't going to blossom?
Who told you that you weren't going to grow?

Your petals are delicate
    Your stem is sturdy and strong

Your thorns to protect from predators and prey
    Your soil is hidden in the richness
    of His splendor

You are noticed in the light even at night
    The Sunlight from His Son
    eliminating schemes and agendas

Allowing you to stand sturdy, delicate, bountifully, and beautifully
strong

You will rise
You will stand

And those surrounding you will marvel
in awe at your beauty
because The CREATOR of the universe

wanted you to be that way
You are a rose even if you grew out of concrete

God has fine-tuned your soil with His

You will stand in the midst of your surroundings, and still be beautiful

All will notice every radiant color and how striking you are
With no attention to the thorns that are there

    Stand beautiful, rose, and radiate the fragrance
    you were created for

Fill Me

God, empty my heart
of anything that doesn't display Your attributes
   KIND -
      DIVINE –
         HOLY –
            PURE –
               RIGHTEOUS –
                  GENTLE –
                     MEEK –
                        HUMBLE –
                           PATIENT –
                              LOVING –
                                 COUNSELOR –

      EVERLASTING ENDURING SANCTUARY YOU ARE!

If we are created to be in Your image
then we are to be Your Sanctuary
in our attitudes toward others
submitting any unholy thoughts or practices unto You, God
to be a vessel honorable at Your leisure for use, not abusing Your
grace for our own heart's desire to use
comforting   HEARTS –
Redeeming the lost
was the price You paid on that cross

Above all, we are to
                             LOVE –

Which is the GREATEST gift of them ALL

Continue to REDEEM my heart
to the true meaning of LOVE
By saturating my

             HEART,
           MIND & SOUL
           With You GOD

You Can't Straddle the Fence

Wounded for our transgressions
Chastised for our peace
Flesh pulled from His bones
He did it for you and me
So, if we would fall, we could get back up
Mercy, grace, and salvation was His goal for us
Someone had to take the blame
Someone who was without blame
No sin, No corruption
The ultimate sacrifice to give us life
Bloodshed to make our sins clean
To wash away all the things that we have done
Is it not apparent to you that He gave his life
For the atonement of you and I

Yet your eyes are blinded with

wrath, greed, sloth, pride, lust, envy, and gluttony

So consumed about only yourself
Your fleshly and worldly desires

Do you realize you need help?
What does it profit a man if he gains the whole world
and loses his soul?
Hell has no age limit
It accepts applications for young adults, middle age, or old

satan was defeated thousands of years ago
but he wants to take as many souls with him to go
to a place that is forever torment
No heaven or second chances
You had your opportunity on earth
You were good in the sight of men
But behind closed doors, you did dirt
Temporary pleasures only last a brief time
But God's love is eternal, it never has an end

(continued on next page)

Even when you are walking in unrighteousness
He loves you even then
But never take advantage of grace with your sins
God holds the remote to your life
He can bring it to an end

What will you say once you die and you are in front of our Creator?
Begging *Lord, let me in*
You would think it's messed up if He says

Depart from me due to your sins
You never took heed of my call
You never took heed of my signs

Repent now, allow Jesus into your life, forget sin
His love is so much more important than your worries,
and false praises up to Him
Let go of carnal things that hold no eternal value
You can't straddle the fence
Either you are for God, or you're against Him

There are only two kinds of people
First is the kind who are saved and follows Christ
Second is the kind who aren't saved and follows the devil
There is no in between

> **Matthew 6:24** - *No one can serve two masters. Either you will hate the one and love the other, or you will be devoted to the one and despise the other. You cannot serve both God and money.*

There is no in-between
No third choice only one of the two
So choose this day whom you will serve
God gives us the option to repent
He gave His son Jesus Christ for you
Will you accept Him in your heart?

I'm Just a Girl

I'm just a girl Born into a world based on money, sex,
and infatuation with physical appearance
Or a reality show like Desperate Housewives

The world's most famous celebrities
But what have any of them done for me?

Nothing but polluted my mind once upon a time
with words and emotions that seemed to have
some type of effect on my life
and perceptions of things

I was occupying my mind and wasting
time objectifying myself to what I was
hearing, seeing, and ingesting into my soul
Which, in return, affected my way of living

So I threw all my Cd's out of my window
while driving down La Cienaga one day
I was tired of pouring sad songs into my spirit,
that wasn't helping my soul
but had me in some kind of trance

The whole time I should've been listening
and seeking Jesus Christ!

But who will listen to me?
Who will listen to me as I pursue Him?

The one who rose from the dead in three days
Who was beaten and bruised
for iniquities to reconcile all that was lost,
giving hope to mankind

But what can I say?
I'm just a Girl

Look Ahead

You may think you've done too much
for Him to clean off the slate

You might wonder if He will forgive you this time
Stay out of yesterday because God is not there

Look to the promises that lie ahead

For His blood was shed
For His blood was shed

For He paid the price for you and me
Your sins and your iniquities

Look ahead

Grandma Z

Growing up, I remember the way you would sway from left to right
every time I would come and spend the night

You would tuck me in tight
I didn't understand too many things as a child
besides mama telling me that you would drive some miles
so you could hang with me

You'd pull up in your big long Cadillac,
jump out dazzling in your bling and gold
Made sure you gave me a few dollars to fold

God-fearing woman who never acted sickly or old,
I enjoyed the time that we spent together
But I lost track of time, assuming in my mind
that you would be here for a lifetime

How un-clever and selfish of me
even though I already knew who has the power
and authority, Christ Jesus

He's in control of all things, including you and me
I realize that it's only normal for me to cry

Though I'm strong spiritually
I'm still a human
I realize we all have an expiration date
I'm sure going to miss your pretty green eyes
and beautiful face Grandma Z, tell Jesus I said hi

As you strut your beautiful self, dance
with my great grannies
and beautiful angels in paradise

Grandpa Johnnie

I'm on the Battlefield Fighting for the Lord!
I'm on the Battlefield Fighting for the Lord!

That particular song makes me think of you
All the trips to church on Sundays;
Heading to Sunday school
All the great talks that we had in this life

I am going to miss you, but I will be alright
We prayed together, we laughed, and you always encouraged me
beyond physically, in a way that will last eternally, spiritually

You were one of the strongest and most influential men in my life
regardless of the physical ailments that you endured
You still pushed through and served Jesus Christ

I remember when I got married, you walked me down the aisle
You were sharp as a whistle, and clean as a Mississippi chitterling
with your silk-pressed hair hanging under the bottom
of your black wool hat with the feather on the side

Not that I like chitlins, but anybody that knew Johnnie Thunder,
knew that he dressed so sharp from head to toe
with the 3 piece suit, matching hat, and the shoes to go

It's funny because I will never forget when I was a little girl
and Grandma Z used to hand me like 1, 2, or 3 dollars sometimes
when I used to come over then you would look over your shoulder
to make sure she was gone,
hand me one of those crisp, long, 20-dollar bills

O Grandpa, you were always so smooth,
loving, and real

I will never forget the laughs
When Grandma Z and you would fuss,
and Grandma would say, she was gone get her pistol
and shoot you

and you would say go on somewhere Z,
ain't nobody got time for that foolishness you do

But besides all the laughs and talks, I am confident
that you have entered those pearly white gates
and that I will see you one-day
dwelling in your eternal resting place
which I know, for sure, far exceeds
the physical beauty of this place we call earth

No more suffering, no more tears
No more crying, no more pain

You're in a place where you have stored
your eternal inheritance, which will never perish
all that you've gained standing around the throne,
enjoying the presence of God, The Father,
and our Savior, Jesus Christ

I love you, Grandpa Johnnie

This is not the end
It is right in my spirit
that we will meet again

Grandpa Johnnie & Grandma Z

We need You Holy Spirit

We need You, Holy Spirit
We need You in our lives
Sometimes we tend to go left
When we know we should go right
Yes, we can jump, we can shout, we can scream

But what difference would it make if no one is obedient?
We hear Your voice
Yet we are left with a choice
Why couldn't life be easy and breezy?
Just like a cover girl, I figured it out
because we were not formed nor created
to be of this world

Your word says to come out from amongst them
and be ye separate and Holy
Then why do humans get so caught up
and think that they have the authority?
No, they are wrong
No man was created to be in the image of the world
but in the image of God
Then they act surprised, and they try to hide
in disguise, which leaves their souls left with a feeling of being empty
deep down inside
Some are selfish and full of pride to go to God
and say,

> Lord, give me the Holy Spirit
> so I don't have to shell myself with an exterior
> of carnality

God the son was brutalized
to secure us spiritually

His flesh was wounded for our salvation
His flesh was wounded for our sanctification
His flesh was wounded for us to be able to fall down
in life, to have His Holy word to know what is right

His flesh was wounded, and unfortunately,
some souls are still lost
How could they be God?
After You sent Your son to die on that Holy cross

You lead us to follow You
You are the truth and the light
You gave Your life
For flesh fights with the spirit
Our spirit is willing to surrender to You, Lord
Grasp on to Your word, For it is sharper
than any two-edged sword
We have the access to be baptized and repent for our sins in the name
of Jesus Christ for the remission of our sins,
and we shall receive the Holy Spirit

> **Acts 2:17** *and it shall come to pass in the last days, saith God.
> I will pour out my spirit upon all flesh; and your sons and your
> daughters. Shall prophesy, and young men shall see visions, and
> your old man shall dream dreams.*

You gave this to us but the world acts like Your word
isn't enough
Men put on fake exteriors, which is pride
as if they are so tough and their grace is sufficient
Because people want to believe that they are superior to God

Holy Spirit guide us
Lord, encamp Your angels for protection beside us
The hearts of this world have been turned to false
worship & praise
Pastors and preachers condoning secular behavior
in the Church in these last days

The world needs healing
They need uplifting
They need to submit

(continued on next page)

Allow their flesh to be completely dead
from sin
For it is sin that separates us from being able to connect
to the Holy Spirit

So here is my heart
Here is my life with no Limits
Do what You must because we need Your Holy Spirit
I cannot imagine a life without You

It's Hard to Let Go

It's hard to let the thoughts go,
lingering De Ja Vu memories of me and you
It's hard to let go
because I wanted you so bad
I wanted to love you, and you love me
I wanted that picket white fence
I wanted us to be forever
I wanted to carry your kids
I wanted us to grow gray hair together
Even though it was just my imagination
running away with me, knowing it was
too good to be true

Inadequate Behavior

It's so inadequate for me to behave this way
Shaking my bosom
Letting my hair down
Putting on my best perfume
So when he sees me, he will look my way

Striving to be noticed, taking too much time
putting the pieces of my life together on the outside
while forgetting about me internally

Layering myself and betraying myself
with the attraction of beauty

That a carnal, narcissistic, egotistic,
materialistic man would strive for

But the reality of that reality
would be: is this man a follower of Christ?
Are my external ways affecting
my internal ways?

What you expose yourself to,
what you see, what you hear,
what you consume, has the possibility
of shaping what's inside of you
All these things I know, yet I continue
to feed myself with the sins of the world

When as much as Jesus has done for me,
as much as God has brought me out,
I should continue to have His word
as my daily route, which beautifies me on the inside out

Psalms for breakfasts
Ephesians for lunch
Proverbs for dinner

This is the way that I've learned to abide by
so I steer away from behaving inadequately

I die to my flesh
    I repent
    I cry out
    I call on
    His name

I know the things that I have done
that were wrong because I read
Your word daily, I put it deep down in my belly
so I know what You expect from me

I am Your child, though I've left Your side
to run free and wild
You still choose me

The road to eternal salvation isn't an easy one
You have to stay on your toes 24/7
That's why God sent his son Jesus
to die for you and me so we can be free from our sins,
free from the ideals or labels that the world tries
to put on us

To know that we have the will
to fall and get back up
So go on ahead
Dust your shoulders off
Dust your feet off and get back up
Don't allow temporary downfalls
of inadequacy to get the best of you

Infatuated with being Intoxicated

Infatuated with being intoxicated

Yeah, that was me
Every time I would go to a club or party,
I would have to have drinks
    Shot,
    after shot,
    after shot!

I mean, why not?

I just wanted to get loose
as in open, which allowed demonic doors
to open into my life

Some people say it's just a drink
But after one drink, you might have another drink,
and they start to make you think

Hallucinate
Have uncontrollable emotions
Do things that aren't normal

I never took the time when I had this infatuation
to read the Bible and see what was mentioned
about this type of infatuation

It says in
    Ephesians 5:18 *Do not get drunk on wine, which leads to de-*
    bauchery. Instead, be filled with the Spirit

Meaning the spirit of Christ Jesus,
not the spirit of lust
A lying tongue,
feet that are quick to rush to evil,
a spirit that causes physical encounters
with other people, changes in characteristics
under the infatuation of alcohol
will have you completely out of your normal self

Sometimes you get so drunk you get lost, and you have to call for help
Not to mention the damage that it severely causes to your liver
15,000 people die from alcohol-related diseases and issues every day
People walk right out of the club, jump into their cars
and drive, without fear

Therefore, being intoxicated causes daily
in the U.S., 30 deaths
That turn's out to be 1 death every 48 minutes

All this because people don't know their limits

First and foremost, being excessively intoxicated
is opposite to God's word

Second, you're not obeying the laws of the land
Doesn't The Bible state to obey those in authority
over you? So if you're tryna get drunk
        Get loose
        Hang out
        Have fun

or whatever you'd like to call it, observe
your consumption of alcohol

Better yet, why do you even need it?
I highly doubt that if you picked up a bottle
of booze you'd even read it

You'll notice on there after you read through
all that nonsense and Jibber Jabber
That it says Spirit

Because unfortunately, marketing companies
will never tell you how a large consumption
of alcohol truly disrupts your spirit

My Invisible Sword

Sometimes I carry this invisible sword
that you cannot see
in my attempts to fight certain battles
that I should deliver to my King

Graced with His love, yet I was consumed with fear
of timidity, comparing my life to others, saying

are You sure God, me?

I've got too much going on
Who wants to hear me?
My life was shattered into pieces

are You sure, Lord me?

My lips are not eloquent enough to deliver
messages to kings and queens

My words are plain, once shaken,
derailed from my destiny, I'd say,

Lord, are You sure of me?

I fed into Satan's lies that my life
is of no worth and your family is cursed

Who would listen to me?
But The Lord God's almighty spirit prevailed
and unleashed His word of truth:

Daughter, give me your sword
Let me give you your crown
I fight for you
  Listen now:
  You speak for me

You do not have to carry a sword
of defense to cope where you are,
just carry Me

My words of truth are filled with more power
of validity than what you believe

  Be gentle,
  and humble,
    yet assertive
    and confident
Be giving, loving, plant seeds,
sow, reap, water,
mature, grow

Most importantly, surrender
your sword for now to Me

At times you will need it,
but this fight is on Me
I want you to be think before you speak
and be careful in your speech

Surrender your sword
and remember to rest in Me

Compton Courthouse

I wish I could sugarcoat forward-slash filter this
I wish it was no barrier

Unfortunately, it has been
Had fights for my life at this courthouse

Don't have enough fingers to count
Filed restraining orders

Declaration of divorce
He threatened to kill me if I ever left

Self-help desk
Hours spent in this courthouse

You would've thought I was on paid staff
I couldn't even afford to park

So, I Parked on the streets,
caught buses in front of this courthouse

Witnessed a drive-by shooting
in front of this courthouse

Had to drop to the floor
Prayed for people, gave them

The Gospel so many times
in front of this courthouse

I witnessed the history of revolutionaries
fighting for rights in front of this courthouse

Walking in peace & unity
Liberate the people:

(continued on next page)

Lynwood Cali native
Ralph J. Bunche & Enterprise Native
Willowbrook projects native

Don't tell me this City ain't no good
Don't tell me voices don't raise out of this City

I know 3 sisters that lived here
1 speaks 3 different languages
1 does martial arts
1 has published books

I know teachers who built schools from the ground up
I know Pastors who have transformed lives here
I know Mayors who implemented changes
I know myself who was raised by a single black momma

My father was incarcerated
just about my entire life

I've had several mental breakdowns
Can't even count the number of times
I've been in an ambulance

Now I'm a business owner
I have a record label

Worked for multimillionaires who entrusted me
to write checks and make deposits

Now I'm learning how to write grants
I've published poetry, music, and books

501 (c) (3) me
My heart is for God and people

Shifting hearts by the power of Christ
By the healing and deliverance, He has brought me

Sharing my songs of victory
Sharing my voice with what God has given me

Don't tell me voices don't raise out of this city
Don't tell me that if you've fought court battles, you can't do great
things

Voices raise out of this city
Mines is one of them

Music

I am the sound that sends chills down your spine
The rhythm that sends vibrations through your legs
I am the movement beneath your feet

    Feel the rhythm
    Feel the beat

I am the acoustic guitar
I am a base 808
I am a drum
I am strings
I am chimes

A sound that never gets old
A melody that you can't forget
A song that you play on repeat all day long

    Can you feel the rhythm? Can you hear the beat?

I am a voice that is so beautiful,
the one that makes you cry

I am a, La, La, La in the middle of the day
I am poetry over a beautiful melody

    Can you hear the rhythm, can you feel the beat?

I am a lullaby sound
I am keys
I am poem
I am rhythm
I am instrument
I am a song that you will never forget
I am the sound that you love to hear
I am a symphony within your soul
I am Music

Gratitude

I can never say thank You enough
You're so graciously kind
You love me so much

You awaken my soul
Your word renews my mind
Changing my life, one day at a time

The oceans, heavens, and trees
sing glory to Your name
Your love is eternal

Your love never changes
With gratitude, may my heart
and life be in service to You

The only living God
who is faithful, unwavering,
merciful, persistent, and true

God's Love

It's God's Love
That is Love
Heartbeat
Molding me like clay
The Potter's Hand
Your Sacrifice
Gives me life
JESUS Christ
Cool Breeze
JESUS, You are my heartbeat
Forming a love in me that last eternally

> You are Love
> You are rhythm
> You are cymbals

> Keys
> Strings
> Pen Drop

Sweet Melodies from Heaven raining on Me

Fill this place in my heart
Fill the hearts of Your people

Your love is enough
to heal every heart

Words

Who will you share it with?
Who will ever witness it?
If you keep it bottled in your mind,
it will stay in a cluster of possibilities

In old torn notebooks and journals
on shelves collecting dust

In your phone notepad
On your laptop

Free it
Free your words

Someone needs it
There may be someone's dreams wrapped
in the releasing of your words

Don't keep them hostage
Somehow, someway, believe they hold
a purpose that's bigger than you

That must mean something, right?
After all, God gave them to you

The Garden

I rest in The Garden
I have peace in The Garden

I have laughter in The Garden
I feel God's presence in The Garden

Creator of The Garden
Equipping man's hands for stewardship over the Garden

He silences the voice of negativity as the trees,
herbs, and flowers visually silence me as I awe

upon their beauty
Cherubim & Seraphim guarding

the entry so I am safe
Whom shall I fear?

I don't recall the wicked
God has them in a number

He lights up pathways and roads
with narrow paths to Him

A never-ending abundance
of His greatness

Butterflies dance
Nature sings songs

Reminding me I am home
Trees postured up in worship to Him

Uplifting my spirit
Hearing from God in quiet moments

I'm free to be me
Toes in grass

(continued on next page)

Flowers of many kinds
Vegetables
      Fruit
      Herbs
      Spices

Speaking to me from every corner, awakening
my senses to God's perfume

God says quiet, and listen to Him speak
His voice so peaceful, so at home

Walking and sitting with Daddy God,
carrying me in His arms

The Garden is that secret place
Waiting for it to be restored 100%,

as I press toward the mark
during my time here on planet Earth

Please Excuse Me

Please excuse me
if I walk into a room with my head up high, smiling ear to ear
No lies are needed, nor hypocritical false religions
intended to appeal to your conversations or opinions

Please excuse me
if I am confident, bold, passionate, and in love
with the fact that I am in love with the one who loves me back,
whose sovereignty is above every mortal, whose competence
can't quite grasp the fact that we have a ruler
who desires fellowship with His creation

Please excuse me
if I jump with joy, raise my hands to the sky,
utter words unknown to man, and sing praises
to the name of Jesus because He has done great things,
and I love Him

Please excuse me
that I may not take notice or be fascinated
by your attempt to wow me with your
Ooos and your Ahhhs and your focus
on prosperity stating God's got a blessing for you
when we should be focused on

God got a lesson for you
He desires your heart, your praise,
obedience, the fruitfulness of His commission,
discipleship, purpose, and mind

Please excuse me
that I choose not to entertain your canards
or conversations about dispensational concerns
or beliefs that are opposite and contrary
to God's word

(continued on next page)

Quoting constantly, "I'm saved by grace, God knows my heart."
So that you can feel temporary relief
of adequacy to justify your doing of whatever
you want and loving the world above God

> **Matthew 22:37** *Jesus replied: "Love the Lord your God with all*
> *your heart and with all your soul and with all your mind."*

There is a specific reason He wants us to do this

Please excuse me
That I'm not striving to be a millionaire,
drive a big fancy car, roll with big celebrities
or stars, turn up, get faded, or even get it in

There's no need for me to pretend I did those things
in the past when I was living in sin,
which ultimately left me feeling hopeless and empty

Temporary fulfillment can only get you so far
I thank God for grace and forgiveness

Please excuse me
That I'm not worried about how short
her skirt is or what she has done in the past
I'm just grateful that she is here
Our job is to uplift and speak the truth
in love

Plant the seeds in the soil, they will grow
in due season on God's time, not ours
Remember, we are the branches,
and God is the true vine
Allow your spirit fruit to reproduce
the light of God in you
To be an example of what is appropriate for God

God has no respect of persons
He loves us all the same,

Please excuse me
that I am conspicuously displaying
my affection and adoration for a Savior
who endured our transgressions to prevent us
from being in an ordeal of eternal damnation,
yet some Shepherd of His body continues
to recite and give watered-down partial reports
of God's mandate in their sermons....
Because they are more concerned about appealing
to the perceptions and opinions of those whom they Shepherd over
They wouldn't want to displease their council
It appears to me that the Shepherd of the body
should be striving for total submission
to God's will, not men's

Sometimes titles, positions, names,
and beliefs are backward's and insubstantially
vague to the motive of God's truth
which is vigorously displayed
in the B-I-B-L-E

Please Excuse me
that these are just my opinions and beliefs,
don't quote me or judge me due to my desire
to accomplish my Father's divine purpose
by unveiling the truth of reality

These are just my observations of facts
For I am undeserving of receiving an award

I am just a Servant to my Father
For the clock is Ticking (Tick-Tock, Tick-Tock),
I don't have much time to waste
so I must convey the truth of God's will

For the hope and knowledge that there is more
to my life and eternity than attempting to appeal
to people's minds and the world's standards
when my concern is to appeal to Christ

(continued on next page)

I could never express myself enough to compare
to His sovereignty, love, mercy, grace, and goodness
For Jesus deserves so much more
then what I can offer Him in this mere
time of my existence on earth

Thank goodness that His grace
is sufficient, even in our weaknesses

So, please excuse me

Confidence Within

You...
I've been wondering why you've been walking
with your head down when you should
have your chin up
Did you forget?
You are an heir to The Throne
Daughters & Sons of a King
who've been giving authority to...
Trample over serpents to...
Walk on water by just your faith
that you put in Christ
You are fearfully and wonderfully made
Don't entangle your mind with

#livingmybestlife

#goals

#instagram

which can enslave those...
Who put their hope in those frivolous things
because when you're walking with The Father,
that is the #bestlife when He provides
He is the Ultimate Visionary
who gives visions to His people
trust that you lack nothing
You've been given the tools
Your dreams are not in vain
Nor is your pain or suffering
You got this
God got you
While the world is consumed
with the consummation of the bag
We run & press toward the prize and mark
We've got a crown that awaits us, God sets it before us
Faint not, our harvest awaits us

(continued on next page)

You've got favor written all over you
You've got heavenly assignments to fulfill
during your time here
You have territories that need you to war
in the spirit

Inhale and exhale
No stress
Just rest in Him

If we know that Christ went through trials
and sufferings than we, who belong to Him,
are going to have suffering

Don't lose HOPE
Your light shines in the darkness
It cannot be hidden

It is ever so bright for the world to see
No one lights a lamp and puts it under a bowl
Your light gives light to others
because God created you that way

Ignite the fire that resides in you
Your existence is not without purpose
God did not put you here on earth for nothing
You've been destined for greatness

This Love

I've got this intimate love
This love intimacy is healing and soothing to me
Not the type that would bruise me,
misuse me, or last for a temporary time
This love will last an eternity
This love is unconditional
This love is more than physical or mental
It's a spiritual type of love because no flesh
can encompass this kind of love
It's more than just a shining ring on your hand
It's more than just a feeling of sensual ecstasy
This is a love, that is the best of all kinds
because it is love itself
A love that truly stands, not one
where when things go bad,
goes missing and is not there for you
This love takes on burdens for you
This love lets you cast your cares and anxieties
upon its shoulders
This love does not weigh you down but builds you up
and makes you strong
This love brings out the best in you
This love takes you as you are
This love makes you shine from the inside out
This love is from God
This love is God
This love gave its one and only son
Because this love just wanted
to be with you and me

Change is Gonna Come

Trial after Trial
Test after Test
Your spirit indeed is willing
Though you have battles in your flesh

A Change is Gonna Come

Put on the whole Armor of God Because your

Change is Gonna Come

Prepare for the battlefield because a

Change is Gonna Come
Day and night
Night and day

Steadfast to God's word, and pray
the enemy seeks to sift you
and make you hit rock bottom

But The Savior Christ rose in three days
from the grave so He conquered rock bottom
In Him, you can conquer and do all things

A Change is Gonna Come

God rose and rises above every circumstance
Trust that you, as His heir, will rise above too
Nothing can stop you
because what God has for you
no man can take away

It's already done
It's written in His word
God has predestined you for great things
Speak life with your words
Have faith in God

A Change is Gonna Come

Don't get caught up in things only seen in the physical
God works wonders and miracles in the Spiritual

He works wonders even as you are reading
these words
Even as I am writing this which shows
the manifestation of His glory

So Don't Let Go
Because a Change is Gonna Come

Sonship with The Father

I need You
I long to be in Your presence
You are Alpha and Omega,
a King who died to save us

I am Your child
You are, I am,
the beginning and the end

My love, my best friend, You forgave my sins
and never stopped loving me
when I was lost and felt as if I wasn't worthy
of Your love
You kept me in Your love,
despite my actions

I appreciate You correcting me
because I know You only want what's best for me

I choose to follow You
You give life
You are the truth and the way
Let me follow You, Daddy God, all the days of my life

If I look down broad paths or ways
where roads do not lead me to You,
lead me the right way to go

Being one with You gives me life
You created all things
You sent Your Son into this world
to redeem us from the fall
Without Christ, our spirit isn't alive
and our souls would cry
Because our flesh and inner man
can't stand to survive

His word says in

Galatians 2:20 *I have been crucified with Christ and I no longer live, but Christ lives in me. The life I now live in the body, I live by faith in the Son of God, who loved me and gave himself for me.*

He gave Himself for me, and you
What a Father He is

You are the Way

You are the only way
It took me to be in a place
of loneliness, a place of hopelessness,
a place of filth and unrighteousness
where worship was my only option
Covered and shielded by uncontrollable emotions
when my emotions needed to be focused on You

I felt washed up and abused,
didn't think that I was no good
and of no use, but You showed me Your light
so I had to stop my internal fight
Your light is so bright that it shined
in through my dark life

Despite me
You loved me

So may my praise be as oil to Your feet

Because You are the light of my life

You are the way

Beautiful Surrender

Found Myself complaining lately and not being grateful enough
then The Holy Spirit reminded me to let God do His job in my life

It's Your Story, Eboni, I understand said, God
But it's really Mines because I'm the one writing it

Uncomfortable about my position, not grateful
for the things I do have, and all the blessings
God has given me, yet, desire all the things
I feel I should have, spending too much time
on Social media or Google, trying to identify
all my concerns with questions such as,

> Do I have a problem?
> What does this mean?
> What does that mean?
> What's the meaning of this?

When God has graced me with His love
time after time, showed me mercy, love, and kindness,
pulled me out of the lion's den,
and showed me that He cares continuously
regardless of my shortcomings
and unwise choices I've made
in my life thus far

Daddy God, You know my heart
Please clean up the ways
I hold hostage that are unpleasant to You

Sometimes I get so tired of trying to keep going
but I know You love me and want what's best for me
You want to prosper me and let Your Holy Spirit permeate my
soul

Take up that space, God, where the voids are
without Hope, without Joy, without Love
So that my eyes & heart can be fixed on You
That is the only way that leads to joy and peace in You
Beautiful Surrender unto You, Lord

Freedom

There is a freedom that God gives
There is a peace that He brings

There is a song of joy that lives within
when you dig deep and let God in
that song sings loud

Giving unity to brothers and sisters
Giving you a strength that frees you from the lies

You can proudly stand with grace and poise
with awareness of God's truth

This is truly who you are,
truly who you were created
and destined to be

God was intentional
Transformed you are internally

Count it all joy
You are not defeated

God's promises are not void
He fulfills them

Victory is your portion and so is freedom
Songs of joy you shall sing
Songs of peace

God's grace is sufficient
You are not in bondage
You are free

Angry

Silence me quickly
My blood is boiling to the top of my head
A tea kettle ringing to its highest pitch
I want to fight someone in my attempt
to be slow to wrath, swift to hear,
and slow to speak
for the wrath of man does not produce
the righteousness of God
Honest to God truth, I don't want to hurt anyone
I know I was created to love and walk
in the fruits of Your Spirit
        Patience, longsuffering, forbearance, forgiveness,
        and all of that good stuff

But honestly, I'm losing control and pushing myself
to a breakdown like a gas tank on E,
stopping on a freeway
I know Your word says to be not quick to anger
and do everything in love
Right now, I don't feel like loving
I don't want to be touched
I don't want to listen
I just want to do what I want
My life circumstances are not all I expected them to be
but, in my reminders of who you are,
I'm reminded that everything will work
according to Your purpose
So I inhale and exhale on Your promises,
gasping them in like a walk amongst the most beautiful
shoreline on a perfect beach
Having to walk away because I don't want to lose control
Pacing with fast-paced strives to calm my spirit down
The feeling of cool air on my face,
which reminds me to slow down the rage within
Gazing at the sunset over the horizon of Your ocean
Bringing to my remembrance that everything is ok
I almost forgot that You are in control

(continued on next page)

I believe that miracles can happen overnight
I'm trying not to lean not to my own understanding
Because right now, it's hard to receive it because
I'm fighting to believe it will happen for me, but,
I'm supposed to trust in You with all my heart
My heart is faulty right now
Truth is, I'm scared right now
My heart is aching because
I honestly need You to take over
I need You to guide me
I need You to lead
I'm tired, and I need to slow it down and rest
I need to remember that there's a time
for everything
Right now, at this very moment,
I need to rest on and in Your promises
that You are with me wherever I go,
in my coming in and going out
So I Selah, inhale, exhale,
and breathe in Your truth,
speaking it over my life

Over my frustration
Over my rage
Over my anger
Over my fear

You are my comforter
May Your spirit rest on my shoulders
in my weakness, assuring me that it is well
and I don't have to act in anger

Heaven

Your love awakens my soul
Impressing on my heart and soul, Zion
A place where lost hope is restored
A glorious place awaits, unlike the trials
that have attempted to weigh me down
I press towards the mark
and the prize to receive my crown

Waiting at Your gates to enter in
Angels crying, Holy, Holy, Holy

Lives transformed
No flesh can enter in
Free from sin
Free from hurt and pain
Stored my treasures in heaven

O, it awaits me
A glorious eternity to see
My storage is in heaven where moths
and ravens cannot diminish fine golds and linens
A place where tears are never cried,
just joy

Colors are poured out beyond the sunset,
an array of colors that the earth
has never possessed

I know a place
It's a place called heaven
O, it awaits

Still Small Voice

Fettered chains shackled
around my legs

The light of salvation, hope, and grace
takes the key to remove chains
from my legs

God's wind breezing crossing my spirit,
reminding me of His still-small voice
whispering

this, too, shall pass
I'm building you stronger

The Miracle Worker
Giving sight to the blind

Hope dealer
Giving hope to the hopeless

Fear not
Do not be dismayed
God's holy army is slaying the lies
of defeat

You are victorious
Stand on His word
Abide in Him and watch
the miraculous power
of His healing love
and power work in your life

Don't Listen

he be roaring,
seeking to steal your destiny

Don't listen

Lying about who you are
the father of lies
Sometimes he comes in disguise
Deception, Deceptive, he just wanna get your attention
and point you in a broad direction,
leading you out of God's will,
God's witness protection,
and in covenant with him

Don't listen

he will have you forgetting
who you really are
Don't you know you were born
to do great things and that God
has given you faith to be a shining
light and beam?
God gives you strength and peace

Keep your sanity and your dignity
in your pocket

Don't listen to the father of lies
who comes to steal, kill, and rob you of your peace

Hear and listen to the voice
of The Father of Truth,
the one who gave you your heartbeat

(continued on next page)

Take a deep breath

Reset
Reflect

Let Go and Let Abba Father do His thing
because if your pulse is still beating
trust you are not without purpose and meaning
God's trying to get your attention

What do you think salvation is for?
It is available for you
Close the door to that foothold
that won't let go of you
It cannot break you

Don't listen

Get Jesus in your spirit and kick
the father of lies out of your head

You have a life to live and you will do it
with holy divine intentions, direction,
discretion, discipline, and protection

So don't listen to the one
that tells you that you don't

Revived

Hem of His garment
will make you whole
Eyes opened, and you are aware
of who He says that you are
You can because He did

All lies spoken over you and about you
are in the past

They are behind you
They are dissolved

A submitted life to Abba Father
as the head of your life

Revival takes precedence in your soul,
which makes you whole

What are you Thankful for?

What are you thankful for?
Have you been too busy complaining?

When was the last time you stopped
and thanked God for the air in your lungs?

Have you been too busy being consumed
by your troubles?

Has the constant self-gratification
of your current situation taken away
from your thankfulness?

When was the last time you sat down and spoke to God?
When was the last time you thanked Him for life itself?

Are we thankful for every opportunity we get from God
to give Him thanks for the things He has done already?

What are you thankful for?

Keep in mind and remember,
you are here with me now

You are reading these words
God still has you here for a purpose,

which is something to be thankful for truly
Recognize the cost of the oil on your life

Choose freedom because Daddy God
laid that foundation for you

You are no longer a slave to fear or bondage

Liberty through Him
Men's words or validation do not seek them
Adhere to and heed God's truth
over you, open your ears
You are just a foreigner in this land
So don't expect all to understand keep your eyes on the prize it's
ahead

You see, God speaks clearly, and His voice pierces
the cores of the heart & soul

He surely is alive
Trust He's not dead

What are you thankful for?
His sheep know His voice like a bell
in a silent room ricocheting off the wall with echoes

    Daughters
    Sons

Victory He's already won
Walk in this authority, authenticity, and power
With thanksgiving for all that God
has already done and is set to do

    Unashamed
    Unafraid
    Unapologetically
    With boldness
    No timidity
    Do not fear

God's rod & staff, indeed, are a comforter
which directs and protects us, who are His

Keep this with you always

    His comfort
    His rod
    His staff
    His peace
    His word

Now that's something
to be thankful for, truly

So, I'll ask this question again:

What are you thankful for?

Shine

Letting my light shine with confidence in Him
Creator of the world, the one who knows the stars by name

He knew me before I was formed in my momma's womb
Giver of good gifts

Jesus, the son of God, abides in me, and I in Him
To be rich is to carry His love which flows so deep in my heart

This is the greatest gift of all
It springs forth like living water from my belly

I can't help but speak of Him
Pointing all glory to Him

Bearing His fruit, spreading
an unspeakable joy that surpasses

any pain in my life I've experienced
O, He is my sunshine, and His son shines

Since I am His daughter in sonship, I shine like a city
on a hill that cannot be hidden, carrying

His light with me wherever I go

Put Nothing Before God

An exhort to compel your spirit
I relate in a parallel way

I have had an adoration for temporary
desires in life, based on my own experience

Put nothing before God
For He loves justly and righteously in truth

Put nothing before God
Though He loves justly and righteously in truth

He is jealous for you
He is jealous because He desires

your heart, mind, body, and soul
Your life with full devotion to Him

He wants your fellowship and relationship
This requires communication with Him

When was the last time you actually sat down,
tuned out all the noise of the world,

and spoke with Him? What relationship could
ever develop and grow without spending time in it?

Put nothing before God
Love the Lord your God

with all your heart, mind, and soul
Whatever you invest more

of your time with,
there will your heart lay

Where is your soul?
Where is your heart?

Where is your mind?
What are you putting before God?

Something has taken the place
in your life that He is supposed to

Put nothing before God

Eboni Echols

I'm Scared to Love You

I'm scared to love you
My heart is scarred with stitches in it,
hanging on life support

One more break and it might
just be damaged forever, might not even make it

Not even surgery could repair
the damage to its arteries

Fragile, beautiful soul
tainted by non-so-beautiful souls

Whispers literally sweet nothings
to my heart that penetrated thru my ears

I'm scared to love you,
really love you
Nowadays, what is love anyways?

Its true purpose amongst two people
has really seemed to lose its identity

I'm scared to love you
I'm always trying to find any excuse to break it off

Any opportunity to not stay
because I'm scared to love you

It's easier to just cut it off and move on
before you break my heart because that's the normal
seems like, at least for me

Love has been like a splinter that's painful,
yet hard to get the residue out, you need a whole needle,

alcohol, and a lighter just to remove it completely
from where it punctured through your skin

The residue of the not-so-feel-good part
entered my heart and left its spect of share of splinters

No warmth, just ice-cold winters
Love for me has been a stumping of your baby toe

on the corner of your bed,
unexpected pain that shoots up your foot and lingers

A possible jam, you would think, or a fracture
Shoot, it might even be broken,

it hurt so bad for days
If I could, I would really want to love you
with all of me

    I want to be vulnerable
    I want to be open
    I want to encourage,

        uplift, inspire, and be that safe place
        for you as I want you to be for me

Share dreams and visions laying on your chest,
feeling your heartbeat as you stroke my head gently,
breathing you in deeply, desiring the rhythms
of our hearts to sync, writing you poetry of my devout
sincere, undying naive love on sheets of paper
that will never be seen

Better yet, in my head, dancing on a field of flowers
Oh, I'm definitely a hopeless romantic

    Romeo o Romeo, wherefore in the heck are thou?

But I'm so scared to love you anyhow,
so I've stopped being hopeful of love's possibilities,
I'm really scared because I have uncertainties,
questions that I just can't figure out the answers to
I'm imagining that you are scared, too

(continued on next page)

Love for me has been health scares at clinics,
getting tested for STDs because your husband

decided to cheat, giving birth to twins without their father there to witness
their beautiful stages of childhood to this very day

My twin daughter always asking me when will her dad
pick her up to visit, and me, with that silent metaphor

of mommy changing the subject because I'm faced
with the reality that every day

The reality of no time soon baby girl

Love for me has been a punch in the face,
with a black eye which emerged into an ongoing cycle

of back and forth before I finally decided to call it quits
Nervous breakdowns, a.k.a

manic depression, postpartum depression,
psycho-affective, psychosis, bipolar

How many diagnoses before one can discover
that love caused me to house unwanted demons

because the hurt was so detrimental that the tie
pierced not only my heart but my soul?

I'm scared to love you

But my question for you is if you could
really give me all of you, what would that feel like?

Would our love synchronize in unison?
That it outweighs our fears of being scared?
Giving each other what we truly need
and were created for at the beginning

of the creation of Adam & Eve before the fall?
If it was within my control and ultimately,

I could choose, I would love with all that I could
That kind of love would drive away even

the thought of me being scared
But if the love is not returned, then I have every reason

to be scared to love you
It would be too risky for my heart

It would be too risky for my soul
So I'm letting go and choosing to let God love on me

As my heart and soul are delivered from the false
narrative of love, or the perception

of what I assumed love to be
I'm not stating my story or experience of being scared

to love you for sympathy, I'm sharing this so you can see
my transparency because, honestly,

I'm believing and trusting God to heal me
I have had my share of trials

I have had my share of struggles,
even throughout my journey with God

But in the midst, I still chose to believe,
believing and hoping that one day I will

no longer be scared to love you, believing
that my heart will be 100% healed

with God's true meaning of love, for He is love

As Abba Father goes to my inner being
and performs surgery, just as he weaved me together

(continued on next page)

in my momma's womb perfectly with His healing love,
eliminating my fears of loving you

I only want the love
that He is in

It's the only love that gives liberty
It's the only love that gives peace

What I felt

Love -a strong emotion of regard & affection

Pain - a symptom of some physical hurt

Hurt - damaged feelings or physical distress

Abuse - treat (a person or an animal) with cruelty or violence, especially regularly or repeatedly

Emotions - mood, temperament, personality, disposition

Crazy - brainsick, affected with madness or insanity

Sick - ill affected by an impairment

Marriage - the state of being voluntarily married. Joined for unity

Separation - the state of lacking unity

Family - a social unit living together

Divorce - disassociation, part, cease or break the association

Time - the indefinite continued progress of existence and events in the past, present, and future regarded as a whole

Change - make a difference, cause a transformation

Baby - a very young child, especially one newly or recently born

Effort - a vigorous or determined attempt.

Challenges - an objection or query as to the truth of something, often with an implicit demand for proof.

Rain - moisture condensed from the atmosphere that falls visibly in separate drops.

Sunshine - direct sunlight unbroken by clouds, especially over a comparatively large area.

Hope - Hope is an optimistic state of mind that is based on an expectation of positive outcomes with respect to events and circumstances in one's life or the world at large

On-Time

Took a breath and just woke up,
not knowing if I should have run or just spoken up,
but the enemy had me so blinded and fooled
that he took control of my body and my mind,
tried to take my life one second at a time
but God said

I have a plan for you, my child
I have a calling on your life
This is what you have to go through to realize
that I am the giver of life
No man, no woman, nothing but me
Once this is over, you will be a better woman
because you always believed in me,
just wait and see

As the hours of the day were moving,
time was flowing, and people were coming,
and people were going
It was no surprise that I was not me
I was so blinded by so many things
that I thought were love,
it made me insane, did you see?
But the whole time, Jesus never left me
He blessed me with family and friends
who prayed for me and believed in me
I heard an angel call my name and came
to take me home, and God said

you're not done yet
You're not insane
Your work is not finished
You must go back
Go back
Go back, Eboni

Look at all that I've blessed you with
Look at everything that I have given to you
You have so much living to do
You forgot about me for a second
But here I am at your beckoning
To give you life so that you may have it more abundantly
What I put together let no man put asunder, God said
so, I've blessed you with a son
He was an angel that was sitting by me in heaven
I said to him, Zylan, this is your mother
She is such a great woman
She is so loving, sweet, kind, and forgiving
I have seen her tears
I have felt her pain
She asked me to fix it
She loves too hard
I heard her call my name
It hurts me to see her go through all of this pain
So you must go down on earth so she may stand
I promise you will see Me again
The body that you will use is only temporary
But your soul is forever
Never forget me in all that you do
And when you get to earth, tell Eboni
that God said, "I never forgot you"
I heard your prayer, my child
I may not have answered right
when you called, but I'm always right on time

Hello

Hello new day
Hello new opportunities
Hello happiness
Hello joy

I've sat in my somber and depression long enough
Peace and sunshine have been calling my name
I've had enough rain
so tired of revisiting its cold days -
constantly replaying its unwanted visits in my head

So, I'm letting go of the rain
Saying goodbye to it,
leaving it to soak in its darkness
and cold storms

Blessings have been calling my name
from all my sowing of seeds of goodness

Even my tears in darkness sowed an ocean
giving my very last that I could,
causing a tidal wave to hover over
the land before me

Now it's time to say hello to all the harvests
that have been stored for me
That of both my tears and of my hands
because they have both sown diligently
Now ready to reap the harvest of its joy
with expectations of its abundance and overflow

So, hello overflow, I receive you with joy and open hands

Tablets

Tablets on my heart
Tablets on my soul
Sins of my past
Letting it all go

Wondering if He remembers as much
as I sometimes do

Pressing in the goodness,
but still sometimes condemning myself too

Went against some of my very own beliefs,
wondered, wandered, wondering if he was still listening to me

Broad roads lead to destruction
Narrow the path of those that go to Him
I had to let it go
I had to press toward the mark,
but somehow, one thing kept coming
to me, something I did in secret

He said I'm forgiven
It's covered in His blood
I still sometimes wondered
if I was still good enough
for His love

I wondered, was I still His daughter?
I didn't hear Him speak for so long
I couldn't even hear a symphony,
feel the wind of His presence,
or even hear a song

(continued on next page)

Someone had a hold of my foot
Someone had gotten down deep
and planted bad seeds in my roots,
making me forget who I was
A forgotten daughter left on desolate land
For a moment, I let go of my father's hand
Drifted like a prodigal daughter walking
on cracked roads far from shore, it was dry land

Can I please come back home? Daddy God, Please?

I never want to leave again
I was so scared
The wolves in the streets almost took me out

Even the ones that were in sheep's clothing
I didn't even notice

I heard Your voice almost in a whisper
in distance, please come back home
I was naked

Ashamed
Afraid
Scared
Lost
Cold

     I came running to You
Hungry
Thirsty
Lifeless

And You gave me meaning again
as I rested in Your arms

You anointed my dry scalp with oil,
soothed my scars with ointment,
gave me fresh water from Your spring
clothed me in Your finest garment
and even gave me a ring

I never want to leave
Please keep Your arms around me
I never want to stop listening to You
and hearing Your voice
It is the sweetest voice
that I yearn to hear every day

Safe Place

There is a safe place in His arms
A safe place where walls come down
Where I'm free to be as happy as I want to be
Where I rest so peacefully
My safe place

I'm free to scream loud if I want
I'm free to tell every secret
A place where I can cry as much as I need to
The kind where the snot comes from my nose,
and my eyes are puffy the next morning,
no one asking me what's wrong or telling me,
Eboni, be strong, you got this

My safe place

Where His judgment is for my good
Where it builds my character
in the correction of righteousness

What if I just want that safe place
to be a place where I can be ok
to be vulnerable

A place where my tears are watering my soul,
going deep to the core of my spirit

My voice is my plea for what I need from Him
Heavenly language speaking those words
that my flesh cannot, you see

The need for my Abba Father
This is my safe place, you see

His love wiping away the pain
that hides in dark places of my soul
I can let it all go and surrender it to Him
All the dark places
All that I do not understand
and comprehend

My spirit will utter and groan the pain I feel
My spirit is always willing, even
in the moments that my flesh is weak

God, tame me to what You need me to be,
take this hardened corner of my heart
and make it soft and sturdy as You need it to be

I want You to receive the glory
because it is Your story that gives me a place to live,
giving me the reason for my being

You are everything to me
Strengthen me, but don't let me fail

I prevail with You
You are everything I need

Seeking Your kingdom and Your voice is what I need

Everything else will fall into place as I continue to draw
near to You, because You are my safe place

My Keeper

God overflowing in me
God's spirit resides in me, and I in He
Keeping me in His plan for my destiny
Though, at times, I've walked down
cracked roads that were broad,
he remained my keeper
Protecting me from falling
through the cracks along the broad roads

If you knew the stairs I've had to climb
You'd be wondering how I didn't fall
all the way through, you'd be wondering
how come I didn't end it all?

If you narrow in, open your eyes a little wider,
I'll tell you how
            Jesus Jesus Jesus
He'll never leave ya
He is healer
He is protector

A Good Father
      Redeemer
      Fountain of life

I boast in Him because He is my keeper

You will not Fail

Arise
   Awake
      Walk
        Jog
          Sprint

Keep Going you will not fail
This journey has given you the endurance to win the race
This journey has built your character as God saw fit
You are stronger than you think
Your bones are revived
You are alive
It's no surprise that you've made it here

Keep going you will not fail
It's no surprise that the fire within you moves
Sons and daughters
Your voice gives strength to bones
Sight to the blind
Hope to the hopeless
because God's Holy Spirit within you is relentless

**You will not fail
because His love for you never will**

Painting by Janet Hyun (Eden: Promise Tree)

My Garden Tree

Harvest overflow
God's blessing, fruit growing
on my garden tree

Uprooted the dry roots
Refurbished and tilled bad soil
God's rain watered my soul

Penetrating down to under the roots,
giving fresh life
Giving clarity and precision

as to the reason I still exist
The reason my garden tree is still bountiful
and holds a harvest to give away

The locust tried to take over everything
in my garden because the crop is so good
in abundance that there is much to share
God came through like neem oil, governing
everything that is in my garden,
protecting everything that is there

Now my garden tree contains
fruits, vegetables, flowers, and herbs
of many kinds and many colors

No wonder the locust stayed trying
to destroy what's been growing over here

My garden tree will not wither,
for it is in season year around

I can only walk in Gratitude for the foundation
that God has laid in my garden on my tree,
reminding me that His promises never fail

Only God

If they saw the mud that you were stuck in

Only God

They would celebrate Jesus and honor Him with you
when they see your tears of joy

Hands lifted high with many thanks to Him
Words of praise to Him
Heart posture of sincere gratitude

Only God

Only God could lift you out of mud
That is deep and thick

So only God can receive the glory
and honor that He is so deserving of

You are God

You are light to pathways
Oxygen to lungs
Food to the belly
Nourishment to the spirit
Rest to someone's sleepless nights
You are God

My Obligation as A Poet

My obligation as a poet is to communicate to people
in an authentic and relatable way

To touch people in their
hearts, souls, minds, and spirits,
        inspire, refresh, renew, bring joy,
                make them laugh, cry, and heal

My obligation as a poet is to not sit and be silenced
or quiet but speak up for the voiceless, those who have fears
and hidden pain, break generational curses, uplift people
on their worst days

But even on my worst days, still, be vulnerable in keeping it real

My obligation as a poet is to be
        a lyrical therapist, counselor, doctor, healer, preacher, midwife,
        and teacher

        Health to bones
        Nourishment for the body

My obligation as a poet is to write and share,
but most importantly, to not let
what I write in this life go unshared,
sitting, collecting dust when there is much soil
that needs watering and light for seeds to grow

Black Wolf

before I fell in love with you

You took my heart and buried anything
that was left to give intimately

I couldn't salvage the pieces of my heart then,
even if I tried

I trusted you, placed my heart in a box with yours,
locked it and hung the keys around my neck,

initialed your last name as my initials
I thought for sure you were heaven-sent,

I was the rib God took from you to form me
Deceived the hell out of me

I was sure we were destined to be
A fool, I surely was living on the clouds

Swayed by your smiles, prayer meetings,
and moments we shared reading Bible devotions

for couples, praying to the heavens, feeling a shift
in the spirit

You damaged my heart arteries and left me in ICU
I forgot for a while what fellowship with true brothers & sisters looked
like

I forgot for a while what The House of God felt like
I took your ring, planned a date, thanked God

that I no longer was sitting patiently waiting like a good Saint
for 4 years after my last relationship hoax

I wanted to be your forever
I was confident that you were my forever

(continued on next page)

After all, I was doing everything right,
right? Before I fell in love with you, black wolf, you bit me hard

and almost killed me
At that moment, I imagined that I could not go on

as I laid in bed with blood leaking from the wound you left
Thank God that I recovered and found my way

back to the sheepfold, where
my shepherd performed surgery

How I Survived an Abusive Marriage

My life
If I could rewrite a piece of my life
I would've thought twice
About a decision that I made
A decision in my mind at that time
That had me enslaved
I chose to marry a man I had barely known for a year
Because growing up, Mom was just a little bit overprotective,
on edge about everyone and everything
No overnights for me or weekends
at too many people's homes
No camping trips
No parties
She kept her kids close in a safety net
I was afraid to experience things in life for myself
I mean, what can I say?
She did it on her own; Pops was locked up in prison, she didn't have
much help
She did the best she could do
So I decided at an early age
to take matters into my own hands
To get a bit of an escape
A bit of freedom
And marry what I assumed would be a man for me
A man that I assumed I would spend my whole life with
You know, growing old, family gatherings, and carrying his kids
Well, at least that's what I thought it would be
but it turned out that I had become just another statistic
to a black single mother with a baby daddy
It all happened really fast, you see
I was nineteen; I had dreams
I came across him & he was just so charming
And swept me off my feet
I mean he
showed me, love, in so many ways
Flowers, jewelry, helicopter rides,
surprising me with gifts at my job,

(continued on next page)

81

dinner on the beach, 3-hour phone calls
from night to day
It was a feeling of never-ending
butterflies in my stomach
I was certain that I was in love
Okay, so I really felt that he was the one
But the most important thing,
I never got consent from God
I never asked Christ if this was this was the man
that He chose for my life
Of course, we would encounter
much turmoil and strife
So he moved me out of state
He promised my mom he would keep me safe
But five months into the marriage
It was too late
I came back to Cali with a big purple bruise
on my face from knotted type fist
to the side of my eye
My hair was all bald and all over the place
I dropped 20-30 pounds
I felt ashamed and embarrassed, didn't want to tell a soul
I was afraid they would tell it
And say girl, please... call the police!
But I was so naïve
I'd say he didn't mean to hurt me
I was caught up in the cycle of abuse
So I continued to allow myself
to be available for his abuse
Packing bags, sleeping on friend's couches
Then back with him because he just couldn't live without me
Sometimes, I wish he would've just killed himself
since he couldn't, but it was really me
He was killing my spirit
This went on for some years
It took an act of God to finally get help
God put me in a situation where I could no longer control
the situation, nor could I help myself
Mental, psychotic breakdown
Child protective services almost took my firstborn

My soul was broken
It was heavy
I'm grateful that God gave me a heart & soul
that rocks with Him
I heard His voice in a whisper as I lay in bed
3 months pregnant with yet another bruise
across my face, telling me if I stayed, I would surely die
and not be with Him
I'm thankful that God stayed with me and whispered
in my ear when all I could see was death
Even with life inside of me
I went back and forth, back and forth, back and forth
I continued to go to this man
Once my child was born, God opened my eyes
I experienced many trials at the beginning
of my first child's life, but God did it to get my attention
and get me closer to Christ
So yes, God, I changed my life
Yes, God, I will do what's right
I never want to go through another sleepless night
Tossing and turning in a cold room with only a sheet
to comfort my bruised face and my tears
Waking to a man that's supposed to love me
But instead, we argued and fought
Thank You, God, for staying with me
Thank You, God, for never abandoning me
Thank You, God, for renewing my Life, mind, soul, and heart internally
Now I can use my life as a living testimony
Praising and serving God continually for His grace, love, mercy and
for allowing me to survive an abusive marriage

I'd like to be Seen

I'd like to be seen as love
I'd like to be seen as peace
I'd like to be seen as joy
I'd like to be seen as hope
I'd like to be seen as a fresh glass of cool water
I'd like to be seen as flowers
I'd like to be seen as a ray of sunshine
A breath of fresh air
I'd like to be seen as a rose
I'd like to be seen as colorful
I'd like to be seen as gracious
I'd like to be seen as patient
I'd like to be seen as radiant
I'd like to be seen just as God would see me
Fearfully and wonderfully made
I'd like to be seen as illuminating with God's Holy Spirit shining
through
This is how I'd like to be seen

They Expect me to Be

They expect me to be kind
They expect me to be quiet
They expect me to listen and never speak
They expect me to steal
They expect me to not be skilled
They expect me to be weak
They expect me to be strong
They expect me to not be educated
They expect me to live below the poverty lines
They expect me to rise above
They expect me to stay stuck
They expect me to not win
They expect me to give up
Let go
Do drugs
Smoke
Depend on government funding continuously
They expect me to be marginalized into their equation of that black
girl or the N-word
But I'm here to tell you, I'm far from that
So expect me to be that black woman who is amazing and phenome-
nally created by God

Beautiful

Arising to your soprano falsetto melodies to my ears
Beautiful
God made you stand out
Beautiful
Wings spread displaying His design
Beautiful
Even with just a snippet of His splendor
Beautiful
Amethyst purple, sapphire blue, ocean blue, emerald green, opal green, sunset orange, onyx black, russet brown, sun lily yellow
Beautiful

> **Genesis 1:21** *NIV So God created the great creatures of the sea and every living thing with which the water teems and that moves about in it, according to their kinds, and every winged bird according to its kind. And God saw that it was good.*

Beautiful
You sustain me with your beauty
Beautiful
Little bird you are beautiful
Doing your job protecting delicate flowers from insects
Beautiful
I won't let anyone have me think that you are not
Beautiful
God wanted you to be
Beautiful
You stand out so vibrantly
Colors aligned harmoniously
Beautiful
Your visual display speaks songs to my eyes moving to my spirit, reminding me of God's presence and creation:
Beautiful

Good Morning

Sun slightly peeking through the window seal, alarming my sight that
it's time to get up and prepare for the day
Thank God, pray, read over His word, decree His promises over me
Water at the bedside to quench my parched morning throat
I lean over and take a sip
Tighten my laces
Coat on shoulders
Trying to catch the sun as it fully rises in full bloom out the door
I put my foot out the door, step out into crisp cool air
Eyesights of awes of beauty
The palm trees sit in front of my apartment complex so beautifully,
speaking to me
The red plant in my neighbor's window
Misty dew lingering on some withered plants surrounding me
Oh, how refreshing it is
Crisp cold air amongst my face
Neighbors greeting me, *Good Morning*
The stench of incense screeching through windows, swaying across
my face
The beauty of a quiet morning before the world awakes
This is such a delight in its simplicity
It is indeed a Good Morning

A Trip to The Store

Babies crying
Water low
Riding down the street for a trip to the store
Tired, exhausted, fatigued
Head wrap on my head, pushing a double stroller in front of me while
pulling a basket behind me
A trip to the store
Staff watching and following me
What a coincident that the staff keeps appearing on every aisle that
I'm on
A trip to the store
Having to put merchandise right on the shelf in front of me right
where I am standing
Speakerphone ringing in my ear, speaking special codes on the aisle
number I am on
A trip to the store
No one asked me if I needed help
Just all this looking and checking my basket
Looking me up and down as if I'm some kind of alien
I'm just trying to get water and food to feed my children
But here I am, feeling as if I am being visually investigated for a crime
I did not commit
Does my little black babies scare you
Does my headwrap scare you
Does my milk chocolate skin warn you that I am without money to
make a purchase?
All eyes on me just for a trip to the store

African American

They said we weren't good enough
They said we were stupid
They said we couldn't read books
They said we couldn't spell or write
They said we couldn't sit in the front
They said our skin was ugly
They said our hair was ugly
They killed our babies
Stolen from royal soil
Brought to unknown land across seas
Thrown in water across seas
Now we are buying land
Creating businesses
Writing books
Doctors
Lawyers
Models
Teachers
Investors
Reaching the height of our God-given abilities
Royalty traced in our DNA
Leaving our trace
Now they will never forget
We are our ancestor's prayers
We are melanated human beings, created by God

Seaside

Warm sand amongst toes
Tan and soft, with specs of silver shining like a diamond permeating through
Broken shells of pearl white and brown
I might find treasure if I stay a little longer

Emerald blue waves crash softly amongst the shore where the specs shine so bright

I selah

I remember the beauty of Abba Father's creation
I breathe in and I can literally hear and feel the peace of His presence

Can you see it?
Can you hear it?
Can you feel His peace and love all around you?
Can you smell the salt water through the ocean breeze?
A peace of His creation

Not a cloud in sight

Mountains touching the sky
Boats cruising amongst the waves
Seagulls singing their lullaby
Sun kissing the ocean making it glisten like the finest gemstone
Indeed it is a beautiful sight to see
His spirit moved about its face giving it form
Created by God

God Hears You

It's been a minute
It's been a while
I still believe
I'm here at Your feet
I still hope
I know You can feel my heartbeat
I'm silencing myself so You can speak
I still hear Your voice
I don't understand everything that has happened
I don't have the solutions to figure it all out
But You do, Abba Father
All I know is that I always need You, and I love You forever
Thank You for Your angels here on earth, sending me reminders
that You still have a plan and You can hear my supplications

I'm Just Reminding You

You are enough
You are valuable
You are needed
You are beautiful
You are important
You were born for a reason
You were destined to do great things
You have a purpose
You shine like the stars in the sky
Don't let anyone make you feel otherwise

I Wanted Love

I wanted to love and be loved, but love every time for me felt more
like death choking me
Taking my breath from me when all the while, I waited, prayed, and
stayed faithful
to myself in my pursuit of righteousness and waiting on God
At times I felt like my faithfulness was wasted because love kept wrap-
ping itself around my neck

I won't apologize for my somberness
I won't apologize for my tad bit of negativity
I won't apologize for not always keeping it together
I won't apologize for wanting to be loved

My joy was like a radar for broken vessels and stray dogs
My smile when he said I was his answered prayer and God sent from
heaven
God told him I was his wife, when all along, he had a wife I knew noth-
ing of
When all along, he was sent by the devil appearing in sheep's clothing

I don't know when I'll ever be the same again
The audacity of me to imagine picture perfect

You

If you feel like you don't have enough

You do

If you feel like you aren't strong enough

You are

If you feel you can't go on anymore

You can

If you feel that you aren't beautiful enough,
tall enough, or thin enough

You are

Love who God has created

You to be

Because there is only one

You

This is what makes

You unique

There is no one else in the world like

You

Know that

You are enough

Rest

Rest in God
Rest in the fact that God has you in the palms of His hands
Rest in His unfailing love
Rest in His promises because they are everlasting and never-ending
Rest in confiding in Christ because everything has a purpose, season, and reason
Rest because everything will be all right

ℐ Pray

I pray that you know how amazing you are
I pray that you reach your highest potential
I pray that every gift you have is released in your life
I pray that you walk in faith and not fear
I pray that you overcome your fears and that your tears are water to soil
I pray that your dreams become a reality
I pray that you share your gifts with the world because what's inside of you deserves to be seen
I pray that you get through whatever is trying to bring you down
I pray that you know you deserve the best, so adjust your crown
I pray that you know that you are loved
I pray that you do not worry
I pray that you know you can
I pray that you trust that you can
I pray that you tap into your capabilities with your resiliency
Because you are resilient, you are here, aren't you, and you exist with a purpose?
Your life is not an accident
I pray that you know that trials are temporary and joy will touch your heart
I pray that you inspire someone
I pray that I've inspired you
I pray

Notes/Works Cited:

1. New International Version (NIV) Holy Bible,
   New International Version®, NIV® Copyright ©1973, 1978, 1984,
   2011 by Biblica, Inc.® Used by permission. All rights reserved
   worldwide. (Pgs. 1, 6, 13, 18, 34, 43, 87)

2. "Oxford Languages and Google - English." Oxford Languages,
   Oxford University Press, 2023,
   https://languages.oup.com/google-dictionary-en/. (Pg. 63)

3. *Hyun, Janet* "Eden: Promise Tree" www.janethyun.com,
   2022 Author granted permission 4/20/23 (pg.74)